Read-About Science®

# How Animals
# See Things

By Allan Fowler

**Consultants**
Linda Cornwell, Learning Resource Consultant,
Indiana Department of Education

Janann V. Jenner, Ph.D.

Sharyn Fenwick, Elementary Science/Math Specialist
Gustavus Adolphus College, St. Peter, Minnesota

Children's Press®
A Division of Grolier Publishing
New York   London   Hong Kong   Sydney
Danbury, Connecticut

Visit Children's Press® on the Internet at:
http://publishing.grolier.com

Designer: Herman Adler Design Group
Photo Researcher: Caroline Anderson

**Library of Congress Cataloging-in-Publication Data**

Fowler, Allan.
    How animals see things / by Allan Fowler.
      p. cm. — (Rookie read-about science)
    Includes index.
    Summary: Briefly explains how different animals see.
    ISBN 0-516-20797-0 (lib. bdg.)     0-516-26416-8 (pbk.)
    1. Animals—Juvenile literature. 2. Eye—Juvenile literature.
[1. Vision. 2. Eye. 3. Animals—Physiology.] I. Title. II. Series.
QL49.F69   1998
573.8'8—dc
                          97-26720
                          CIP
                          AC

Most animals have two
eyes. Yet they don't all
see things the same way.

Green frog

Great horned owl

Jaguar

Tangerine hingebeak shrimp

3

# How do you use your eyes?

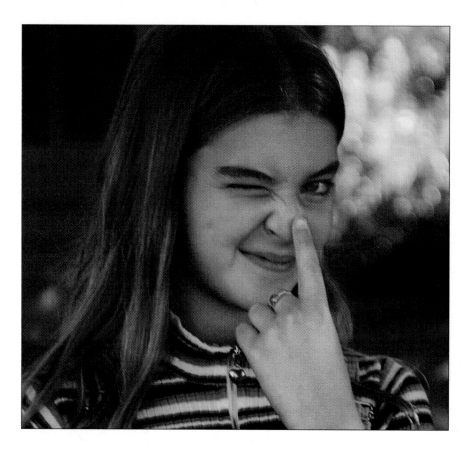

Hold your finger straight
up and touch the tip of
your nose. Close one eye.

Now open it and close the other eye. Did your finger move? Of course not!

It seemed to move
because each of your
eyes saw your finger
from a different position.

When both eyes are open,
your brain puts the two
different pictures together.

This helps you tell how
far away something is—
or how near. It lets you
see in "3-D."

Orangutan

Monkeys and apes see in 3-D, and so do owls. Their eyes are on the front of their heads—just like yours.

But most animals have
one eye on each side
of their head.

Red and green macaws

9

Can you imagine
what the world looks
like to a horse?

A horse can see things
way off to its left and
way off to its right.

But the two pictures
don't come together
in a horse's brain.

Garter snake

That's how a snake
sees the world, too.

Some flatfish have both eyes on the same side of their head—the side that faces up when the fish lies on the seafloor.

Peacock flounder

You see the world in color, but most animals don't. Dogs and cats see everything in shades of gray.

This is how a cat
sees an apple.

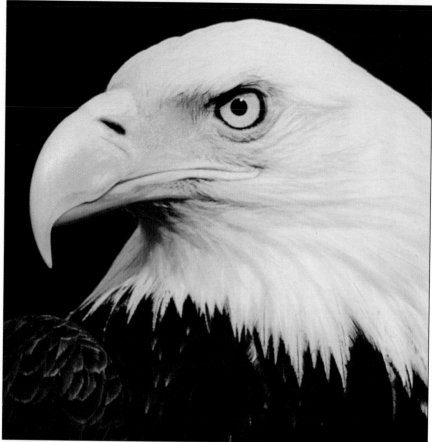

Bald eagle

Some birds see much
better than people do.

A hawk flying high in the air can spot a small insect on the ground, swoop down, and catch it. Owls can catch mice when there is no light at all.

Red tailed hawk

Horsefly

The eyes of insects are
very different from those
of other animals.

18

An insect's eye is made up of many tiny parts.

Each part sees just one small piece of the insect's surroundings.

This is how you see a field
of wildflowers.

This is how an insect sees
the same flowers.

# Fish never close
# their eyes . . .

Harlequin tuskfish

Red soldier fish

. . . because they
have no eyelids.

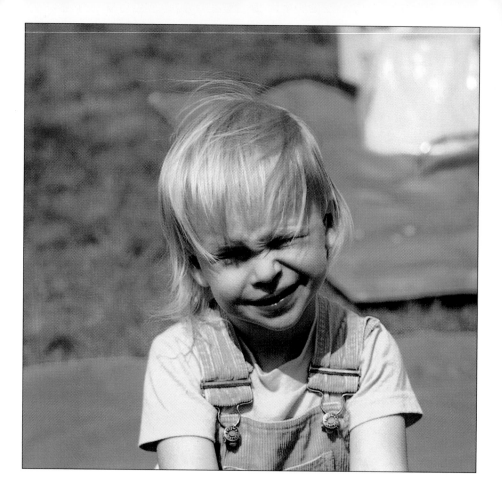

You need eyelids to
protect your eyes.

You can close them
when it's too sunny
or if they feel dry.

Since a fish lives
underwater, it doesn't
have these problems.

Some fish have no eyes at all. They live in dark caves, so even if they had eyes, they wouldn't be able to see anything.

Blind cavefish

Eastern mole

Moles have very small, weak eyes. They don't really need to see well because they spend most of their time underground.

Can you imagine what that would be like? It would be like wearing a blindfold all the time.

People have good eyes
because they need to
see where they're going
and what they're doing.

Aren't you glad your
eyes let you see the
world around you?

You are lucky to see
in color and in 3-D.

# Words You Know

ape

blindfold

blind cavefish

flatfish

30

hawk

mole

owl

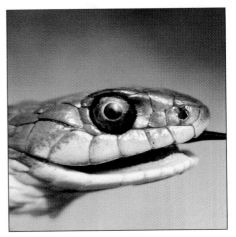

snake

31

# Index

# About the Author

Allan Fowler is a freelance writer with a background in advertising.
Born in New York, he lives in Chicago now and enjoys traveling.

# Photo Credits

©: Ben Klaffke: 5, 6, 29, 30 top left; Ellis Nature Photography: 8, 27,
31 top right, 31 top left (Gerry Ellis), 3 top left (Steve Gettle), 3 bottom right,
22 (Roger Steene); Kjell B. Sandved: 23; Minden Pictures: cover, 3 bottom left,
3 top right, 9, 12, 17, 31 bottom left, 31 bottom right (Frans Lanting);
Photo Researchers: 14 (Renee Lynn), 13, 30 bottom left (Fred McConnaughey);
20, 21 (Oliver Meckes), 17, 30 bottom right (Anthony Mercieca), 26, 30 top
right (Charles E. Mohr), 15 (Jerome Wexler); Visuals Unlimited: 24 (John D.
Cunningham), 4 (Arthur Morris), 11 (John C. Muegge), 18 (Richard Walters).